This Day Dawning
MAURICE RUTHERFORD

PETERLOO POETS

First published in 1989 *26/10/89*
by Peterloo Poets
2 Kelly Gardens, Calstock, Cornwall PL18 9SA

© 1989 by Maurice Rutherford

ISBN 1 871471 07 9

Printed in Great Britain by
Latimer Trend & Company Ltd, Plymouth

ACKNOWLEDGEMENTS are due to the editors of the following magazines and anthologies, in which some of these poems have previously appeared: *Envoi, Iron, Other Poetry, Outposts, Poetry Matters, Poetry Nottingham, Proof, Prospice, Vision On, Weyfarers, Newbury Arts Anthology* (1985), *The Unicorn & Lions* (Macmillan) ed. Moira Andrew, *To Build A Bridge* (LHA) ed. Douglas Dunn.

'The Quiet Men', 'Heinz Gropsmeyer', 'Vagrant's Spring', 'Solatium', 'Ship's Husband', 'Strikebound', 'Painting In Port', 'To My Wife . . .' and 'Sonnet: Through Mother's Eyes' were collected in *Slipping The Tugs* published by Lincolnshire & Humberside Arts in 1982.

The author is grateful to Messrs Weidenfeld & Nicolson for permission to publish 'A Chat With Susan'.

'Bacalao' won first prize in the Bassetlaw Association Of Arts Open Poetry Competition, 1984.

'Pied Wagtails' won first prize in the Ripley Open Poetry Competition, 1985.

'Effects' won third prize in the Newbury Open Poetry Competition, 1985.

'The Bottle Bank' won first prize in the Surrey Open Poetry Competition, 1985.

Peterloo Poets is a list published with the assistance of South West Arts.

The publication of this particular volume was funded by Lincolnshire & Humberside Arts.

Supported by

Cornwall
County Council

for Olive

– who bore the lion's share

Contents

page

EFFECTS

Effects

A mild evening
of a man.
After he died
the daughter came,
A March draught
to his house.

The rooms held
small time
in bereavement.
Doors banged, lino
lifted, silverfish
went under.

Drawers, cupboards
gave up history:
buttonstick, *Sporting Pink*,
gold hunter and albert.
Slippers for the tip,
longjohns to jumble.

His *sanctum sanctorum*—
bellybrace, gimlets,
rabbeting planes—
bought the coffin in oak.
Gift to the Rifle Club
his point-two-two.

The house breathes
fresh, every corner.
Windows stare out
where gnats dance
like fountain balls
at a shooting gallery.

Intake

"... *at o-sixhundred hours tomorrow the bugler will march onto the barrack square; the moment he draws in his breath to blow reveille, I want to see every last manjack of you out of bed* ..."—Sgt. Stokes, K.O.Y.L.I., 10.8.1941.

Soon they had all gone,
senior form idols, conscripts,
volunteers, elder brothers
who had always led the way;
their crowded trains
like millepedes in distress.

Parents and lovers waving
them out of sight, turned,
linking arms into the blackout,
back home without a word.   Gone.
And there was nothing then
for us but follow.

*This is your number, write home
and tell it them, stamp it on
all your kit, your brain,
dreams, turnings in the night;
cling fast to it at dawn;
as the sun goes down remember it.*

We interpreted their trail
of spent cases, jerrycans,
brewed-up tanks and trucks,
closing with an enemy we knew
only as black lines
marked on maps.

No moment, clearly defined,
told us when we shared
our brothers' war,
nor did we think to speak of it
when next we met, strangers
on the far side of years.

One certainty survives:
when the bugler moistens his lips
for The Last Post, those numbers
spring to attention, beating,
by the time it takes to draw breath,
the first chill note.

The Quiet Men

They boast, of deeds performed the night before,
of conquests in dark alleys of their minds,
of gallons drunk and women satisfied,
erecting pedestals and laying claims
on which to build their reputations high
in up-manship and camaraderie.

By day they learn the drills and skills of war,
defile dead ground, find trees with bushy tops
as aids to indication; march at ease,
sing ribaldry and urinate the lanes,
but never ask the question burning deep
beyond the chilling sweat, preceding sleep.

These were the quiet man before they came—
from homes like yours and mine one may suppose,
and on this battle-eve some say their prayers,
and most are virgins if the truth be told;
tomorrow there'll be taller tales to tell
and quieter men for telling them as well.

Interlude

*"Stand to, the old guard,
the new guard's come.
Don't care a bugger
what the new guard's done"* —
but we'll have to imagine the bugle,
the band has moved on to Vienna.
Some of the men, left here
with no longer a war to fight
and not yet allowed to go home,
are assigned to mount guard
over a dump of coal
on the docks at Trieste
—anything to keep up morale.

*"Take me back to Benevento
where the bints are cinquecento . . ."*

Military procedures, duty orders,
the signing of inventories
give way to talk of prices,
going rates and market trends.
Hybrids flourish on the ashes of war:
mercato nero, barter, one currency
for twice its value in another;
chocolate for a child's birthday;
chastity for a perfumed bath;
cigarettes to a dying man with asthma.
The sentry sings, *ad nauseam*, in his box,
a squaddies' version of '*Sorrento*'
against the date of his demob.

Heinz Gropsmeyer

Almost forty years and your name still moves,
shrapnel under the skin, on reflective days.
You were not much older then than in the *Wehrmacht*
photograph above your name, twenty to my twentytwo.
Your canvas pack told more of you—*Kölnischwasser*,
talcum, *Rotbart* blades—though you had not lain
long enough to grow death's beard. More the lad
down someone's street than hated Hun or Bosch
the jackboots made of you.

I tried to pull off the boots, not to ease
your stiff feet but perhaps to please mine
or strip the camouflage from common fundamentals.
I had heard, in school, of your brown shirt,
summer camp and sung devotion to the Fatherland;
in your new fieldgrey, singing your *Horst Wessel* song
could you have heard that we, too, paraded colours
into church for blessing of the same *Gott*
you wore on your buckled belt?

And what of your comrades; he of your own age
unable to rise from his roadside splint, lifting
only his head, inches from my advancing tank,
lest the last bone of blood-let youth be crushed?
And who was he, ageing, who ran through the vineyard
where Charlie took aim, life, and a sickness too?
I remember only the greylined face—and the change
in Charlie—but did not learn *his* name like yours.

Not a month later an ambulance driver
called the likes of you and me lucky
son-of-a-goddam-bitches to get up the front,
and offered to trade his Ronson for my belt that was yours.
The belt I later gave away with other spoils of war
but not your name, *Heinz Gropsmeyer*, it stayed on.
I think of us now, there where you took your *Abschied*,
green grapes under the searing *mezzogiorno* sun;
shrapnel shifting in a distant vineyard's tilth.

A Chat With Susan

(Jacobo Timerman was editor of an Argentine newspaper.
In 1977 he was arrested by the military government and
held in solitary confinement. During interrogation his tor-
ture included the application of electric shocks: these ses-
sions were referred to, by his custodians, as having "a chat
with Susan". After two and a half years of being moved
from prison to unidentified prison, he was released and
exiled to Israel).

Not long in my new, dark place,
a few days perhaps, and nights
I slept propped against the wall,
half clear of the wet floor.

The cell I left had a hole
in the ground through which
to defecate. Here, I must wait
for the guard. Blindfold, I am led

to a latrine I never see.
Sometimes the guards misguide me.
It is their game. Today
they ignore my need and I am

left with my own stench
and the cold, stone floor.
There is a peephole in the door
but I'm not to see it open;

when the guard comes I must
turn my back on the door.
He takes my fouled clothes
for washing, and I see the futile

count of time on his watch
that I once wore. I am naked.
Time is an oppressive thread
stretched between talks with Susan.

Afterwards, there is no pain,
only the endless strand ravelling
and clearing, tightening sometimes
until I think that it might snap.

Today I ask to have my clothes.
They are not dry, I am told,
because it is raining. I search
down the thread for the feel

of rain, and am frightened
by the nothing that I find.
Tonight I am reclothed.
A guard, against the rules,

has left the peephole open.
I peer out into the pain
of light beyond the door.
At first I cannot see, but then

two doors .... a full view
of two doors, a celebration
of space ....
I thought, at first, it was

a trap, your eye watching
from the spyhole opposite.
I stepped back, expecting .....
but when they didn't come

I dared to look once more,
then quickly turned away,
and then.......... again.
And you were doing the same

until we paused, stared,
and shared the silent yoke
of time. You blinked.
I distinctly saw you blink.

I remember, now, that night
we spent together, the strange
game of blindman's buff we played:
peep, and move away . . . .

peep, and move away; our sense
of triumph when we synchronized;
mutual immortality. The love.
Perhaps . . . . . . you were a woman . . . ?

Yes, I clearly recall, once,
just before they came, you rubbed
your nose, slowly, against the peephole,
giving me your caress.

Vagrant's Spring

Dog-rough
he looked,
smelt, felt;
a four-dimensional
jar to the senses.

His tears were
sprung by
primroses.

Solatium

It's only Sheffield plate, she would say,
but it's good and the chasing *is* by hand.
On dull afternoons she would spread old news
on the kitchen table, gather the tarnished moments
of her glinting yesterdays, upbraid them
with a gritty polish cloth blacker in parts
than her hair was grey, and I would marvel
such a dirty rag of cast-off vest
should brighten up her day so.

Stubborn pieces, like leaves on the epergne,
she'd give a harsher reprimand; verdigris
she'd even spit on, indelicately as a woman would.
Always the tray was left till last,
punished with the darkest patch of rag
and more elbow grease than all the rest,
breathed on in echo of orgasmic gasps
and titivated with the floral flannelette
of a long discarded nightdress.

After, humming a tune from Tauber, waltzing,
waiting while the kettle boiled
she would chassé the tray to the light,
mirror its gleam in her face glowing
warm where the copper showed through,
and the canary in its high sprung cage
would start again to sing.
It's only a Roller hen, she would say,
but it's company and it *has* a good song.

Caller From Porlock

Let's talk about such things as warm the heart,
let's draw the curtains, set the night apart,
turn up the central heating and the light;
let's keep each other company tonight.
Let's talk of football scores, the games we won;
that week at Scarborough golfing in the sun
with all expenses paid. Fill up your glass,
let's reminisce to help the evening pass
more quickly.
                Hey, do you remember when
we organized that stag party for Len?
Drunk as a coot you got that night, and he
stayed stonecold sober. Laugh! I can still see
you now, next afternoon in church, your pale
and trembling face white, almost, as Anne's veil,
remember? God, we downed a few that night!

Anne was a smasher, then. I never quite
knew what she saw in Len; but then again
I've often wondered what attracted men
and their respective wives.
                          I'm sorry, Bert,
I talk too much—I didn't mean to hurt
your feelings. Have a top-up, that's the style,
Good Health!
              Now Freda's gone you'll miss her. I'll
say this for you: there's no-one in this town
could say you ever let each other down,
not you and Freda; right up to the end
you always were each other's faithful friend.
And here I go again, *I'm* crying, too;
I have done, often, since I lost my Sue—
let's not decline, when sadnesses intrude,
to give them time our friendship should include.

Let's talk of favourite books; of epithets;
of sheltered housing,
                      crosswords,
                                  launderettes ......

Church Of The Transfiguration

The church has gone.
There's now a block of flats
where spinsters of the parish
changed their hats
for mortarboards
and draped themselves in gowns,
silencing choirboys' whispers
with their frowns;
where altos, tenors,
bases, baritones
sent seismic tremors
through a young lad's bones
when hallelujah choruses
reached heights
he'd never known elsewhere,
on practice nights.

He halts a moment—
sees her standing there,
the choir mistress
sculpting ice-cold air
with chubby fingers,
making evensong
more stimulating
than the vicar's long
soporific sermons—
then he shuffles on
dribbling a snatch
of Handel's *Largo*. One
more bastion
of an old man's youth is down.
A ghost,
revisiting his native town.

Somewhere, Sometime . . .

. . . out of the blue you fall under its spell,
perplexed by knowledge of some sight unseen.
What happens next? Impossible to tell.

You'll know the feeling—suddenly a bell
of recognition rings and takes you, clean
out of the blue. You fall under its spell

and for a fleeting second you can't quell
the thrill of tense excitement, unforeseen.
What happens next? Impossible to tell;

you try to freeze the moment, make it dwell
a little longer; ask what does it mean.
Out of the blue you fall under its spell

but it has gone. Yet sight, sound, touch and smell
can ambush you when you feel most serene;
what happens next? Impossible to tell

however much you try. So prepare well—
déjà vu takes you where you've never been,
out of the blue; you fall under its spell.
What happens next? Impossible to tell . . .

Assignation

It's not, dear Death, that I'm afraid to meet
you yet, but rather that I'd like to be
prepared, you know, leave nothing incomplete,
have time to dot my 'i's, to cross each 't'
and tidy up my final manuscript—
(the sneaking thought occurs that I might then
make late amendments, even have it ripped
to shreds, beg time to write it all again).
It's not that I'm afraid of you at all,
no, just that all the deaths I've known have left
so much unsaid, unchronicled, the small
important things; and guilt in those bereft.
　　I do not ask that you defer my day
　　but Death, do send me first your e.t.a.

SNAPSHOTS IN A SHIPYARD

Timekeeper

Factory-made and tested, he wears
escapement where his heart would be;
seven-day chronometer in sealed case,
shockproof. Robot ahead of his time.

In youth, he was the one who never
questioned that the world was round
or touched to prove the paint was wet.
His monotonous chime today, cliché.

Trusted and ignored, equally, by management,
he is reliable and unintelligent
as a lighthouse, the rock on which it stands,
guarding the Company's stock of hours.

Out and about before the blind of fog
comes down, he anticipates tree-falls,
traffic-jams; the driven snow clears a path
for his car whose battery never runs flat.

He is not caught out by British Summer Time,
depolarized by jet-lag, nor, so far as
the oldest man in the works can recall,
have his grandmothers yet been interred.

Plain fact about him is, his family knows
no crises. He has the fortune of few friends
and, contrary to popular allegation,
documentary knowledge of his father.

Fitter

He wears the coarse cloth cap
of a Russian poet, or a pout-lipped
fashion model; his overalls, untouchable,
reflect the dark like a radar screen.

Most of his tools he has borrowed
and it's doubtful they'll be returned.
You've never seen the badger's bum
he's reputedly as rough as.

You'd not choose him in a shipwreck,
but you could very well be wrong.
Should the lifeboat engine fail to start
or fall apart, he'd be your man.

He'd shuffle the pieces like Scrabble,
rebuild, using four-letter words—coax,
ease the engine into life with tales
of his sea-going time and brothels in B.A.

He does not take discipline kindly. *Rules*,
he repeats, *are for the observance of fools
and the guidance of wise men, take my word.*
You can see facets of yourself in him.

Rambler, angler, wildfowler when he's free,
he knows widgeon and the flight of lapwings,
hears the blackbird writing the score for dawn
above the plainsong of the wind.

Bilge-diver

The acoustics of a double-bottom tank
or smokebox top are Caesar's
Palace to his Sinatra,
his shift-long repertoire
from *Nancy* to *My Way*,
his applause the chipping-hammer.

'Cleaner' is his euphemism,
paraffin and cotton-waste
his daily bread. Filthy,
he crouches beneath floorplates,
bales out the bilges
with a found tin.

He sweats, without change of costume,
through encores, singing to no-one
else listening until, in perfect time,
his cabaret ends with the four o'clock day.
In his bathroom tonight he will cut
a new best-selling single.

Canteen Assistant

She arrives for work by taxi
she and three others
have filled with smoke.

Two years from school her wedding,
pregnant; a stillbirth, the marriage
guttered and went out.

One CSE and *something in catering
perhaps?* her testimonial; ten years on
and she'd like to go back.

She knows far more now of sickness
which keeps her absent from work
less than most of the men she serves.

Bending to the *Bain Marie* she is,
they all agree, more attractive
than when you look her in the face.

Flag days, raffles, round robins
find her an open purse; her smile
is of itself a charity.

She, too, has her dreams, but fears
the thought of her boyfriend's return
from his oil rig in Forties Field.

Her need is not so much sex
as love, and her secret
a week overdue.

Old Book-keeper

It is almost done, this arid stint
of balancing ambivalent extremes;
his life a double-entry system: work
a force-fed virtue, all daydreams debited.

Such are his thoughts these mornings
driving himself to his desk. It's not
so much the job he's going to
miss, as the journeying between.

Company cars with coathangers jostle
him through June and July—past
the bloodied verge where poppies persist
in taking the bend too fast—into August.

Pea-viners have ravaged the night fields,
stripped away the haulms leaving the green
stained soil naked, shameless into the dawn.
The first of the barley is cut, and blanched

straw rolls drunken to a taut horizon.
The sun is poised to drive a slow stake
through the thumping heart of summer.
His odyssey almost complete, he approaches

that place where the man becomes the job,
the job the man; where his aim, now,
is not so much to gain, as not to lose
respect, his Libran grip on things.

And soon he will clear his desk,
pretend not to see the collection
box on its round. He will offer
a loyalty's dregs to the shredder.

Ship's Husband

You don't see his sort any more
except in certain well-worn streets
pushing his bow-wave against the brunt
of years and blowing for a tug.
Tobacco smoke on his meerschaum skin
yellows the cheeks like old charts
of the sea bed, and his rusted brow
is grooved by the warps of time.
He rolls with a list to starboard
through constant drag of sea and net
and, if true to his own dictum, wears
a tarry marline amulet around his neck
against such ills as cannot be cured
by the rawness of onion or rum.
See him riding at anchor at the street end,
or berthed in an hour of sunshine
at an open sham-four door; look
through a parlour window to his past
and see his portrait—by *Jerome*—
in RNVR rig and silver frame
and always outboard-facing, moored alongside
a colour-tinted bride, netted
like a butterfly, ephemeral glamour.
She sees him now the way he was
and forgets to wind forward the clock.
But his memory fathoms greater depths,
lowering a lead-line to sound the seas
of childhood and the chanting school
whose echoing walls failed to out-shout
the sounds of the sea and crumbled
to the running tide of a schoolboy's mind.
He plumbs now the ebb-school hours
of slack-water evening, rippled
by eddies of fish-girls freed
in a clangor of clogs from the oak-chip
smokehouse, where a dozen restless cowls

once swung to the whim of the wind
and a lifetime's talk of splitting-knives,
of haddock-kits and tenterhooks.
Now, heaving in the plumb-line, he returns
to port, to fish-wife's tongue and pummice face,
her busy arms conger-strong and firm.
She, too, in her way, was a ruler of waves.

Sitting by the slipway of his season
provisioning the ship for wintry seas,
hoarfrost whitening his topmast truck, he
fears the black ice thickening his shrouds.

Strikebound

The ship's side gapes,
its unhealed wound still bare;
no caulker's tool
is splitting compressed air.
Where rustblood drips
from yet unplated frames
no pyrotechnic
welders sign their names.

A crane hook yawns
as with the wind it sways
and, metronomic,
whiles away its days.

Painting In Port

What thoughts pervade their separate minds,
these two who share a swaying plank
above the wind and water line
of their rust-measled ship
and paint in shapes of foreign lands,
a red-lead archipelago from stem to stern?

Are they daubing over lives they've left
ashore in a native town whose name
would tumble strangely off my tongue
as Immingham off theirs?
Which brushmark hides nostalgia,
which patch obscures a home?

THE BOTTLE BANK

The Bottle Bank

Rain, all the long night rain
and in the morning clear drops again
fall from the cap of the tall oak post,
course down the painted Pub Food sign
into the uncharitable day.

The back door opens and would close
quickly of itself, but his backside
controls the force of the spring
as he hugs to himself the cardboard box
heaped with the gossip of empties.

His face a perpetual tug-of-war
between grimace of concentration
and a disconcerting grin; his nose
and mouth, like the lachrymose sign,
cannot contain their moisture.

Skirting the pool he could walk through
if he knew its shallowness, the grin
pulls him to the bottle bank,
slides the chattering load down
his belly to his feet and victory.

He selects, with idiotic care,
first clear, then green, then brown,
holds each bottle high in its turn
with his one good hand, a keeper
feeding fish to dolphins.

Each bottle shares its poem with him:
a deal over dinner last night;
rowdy twentyfirst in half-rhymed verse;
arrangement to sleep in another man's bed;
anniversary with only the date to celebrate.

The landlord will give him breakfast
when he's done. Between the grimace
and grin he'll keep the poems' secrets.
He is a man of trust, honourable,
and honoured in his society.

Outlook On Monday

A windscreen glints far off
like a burner's torch, slowly
cutting the country in half.

The swollen hill holds back,
an ocean roller welded to the sky
silent, stopped in its track.

Night's tide has flensed the field,
one sheep down with footrot
hapless, like a stranded seal.

Across the way, a refuse skip
run aground, abandoned.
A neighbour swabs her doorstep,

the clothesline a farcical can-can,
incontinence knickers in chorus
high-kicking out of time.

Pied Wagtails

They invade your thoughts, fuss about
like waitresses to brush away the bits,
flick, pat and tidy up the pasture.

When the sky's this high or higher
you can see, from the window seat, Pickering
sitting, comfortable, in its far fold.

Below the house, in the pasture with the wagtails
gone, they have put up the Michaelmas pens,
unhurried men sniffing the air for rain.

Soon now the trucks, three tiers some,
sheep—sheep upon reluctant sheep;
ramps down to a show of backsides.

Two rough handfuls of fleece and the first
ram performs his *entrechat*, mimicked
by half of the *corps de ballet*.

Green wellington boots, cowpat-coloured suits,
bland bucolic faces; farmers bid for lots,
one against another and the rain.

Drovers, dry in the truck's safe dung-smell,
play cards for cash on the straw-bale, deal,
call, shuffle and reshuffle the pack.

Above, in Wentworth Street and Newbiggin,
chimneys stand the high terraces, sullen
spectators at an end-of-season game.

Misère ouverte. Abundance declared. Suddenly
sun on the roofs. Wagtails mottle the pantiles,
pirouette, reshuffle, bid for unseen insects.

Magazines In A Waiting-room

Two hours morning and evening
they practise take-offs,
landings—circuits and bumps
within a stressed perimeter.

Birds to take attention.
Winging from table to hand
and, restless, back again,
they flutter in front of eyes

that look but do not see. Doves
presaging a pregnancy, vultures
waiting on death; pigeons
homing on repeat prescriptions.

See, they roost now, but watch
them take to the air again
when the mynah calls the next name,
from inside her cage of glass.

Duchess

Not quite yet anachronistic
in a freshly ironed apron,
keeping the dustbin tidy—
the carton of cress
shorn combat-close.
Everyone seems to know her
but few, perhaps, so well
her doorstep conversations.

Her chosen theme today
how the feminine is demeaned
by such as page three
and silly, long-legged girls
on television commercials
who are nothing at all
to do with the product
they purport to sell.

The doorstep edges stoned,
patch of pavement swilled,
she closes and bolts her door
and the street's brightest brassware
completes her daily statement,
her queen's speech,
her early morning protest
to the jeans-and-trainers world.

Neighbours

We greet each other using Christian names
and pass the time of day, though little more.
There's no complaint of children's rowdy games
and not a word about that banging door;

all in the garden's lovely. Well, not quite—
three gladioli hardly serve to hide
that bedspring, those old motor tyres from sight
four seasons round. And who could quite abide

this knicker-buntinged clothesline day by day
and, late at night, departing visitors
who want the world to hear them on their way,
who rev-up engines, double-slam car doors?

Then, when the neighbourhood gets back to sleep
there's always one bright spark on early shift
at six, his valedictory beep-beep
is bloody . . . . well, I'm sure you get my drift.

One irritant we've noticed recently
is where a boy stands at the backyard sink
intent to reach the highest he can pee—
his target is the windowledge, we think.

Beware, this go-go area for dogs
demands that you be careful where you put
your feet, and be forewarned that burning logs
will punctuate your paintwork with their soot.

This sitting on front doorsteps lowers the tone—
sun-bathing on the pavement's just not on—
you'd scarcely think that one would be alone
in wondering where dignity has gone.

But now the movers' men have filled the van,
our house is empty, we're about to go,
the thought occurs: throughout our three-year span
they never told us we'd annoyed them so.

Curriculum Vitae

Not a born leader nor a drop-out, he
is valued for his sheer utility—
state education has prepared him for
the Forces, unemployment, factory floor.

A family-allowance come of age,
they say he's fortunate to earn a wage.
Lucky be buggered! That's his father's shout,
For this we fought—the gaffers, and the Kraut.

He is the basic model as it comes
devoid of extras; he accepts the crumbs
from richer tables and he keeps his place,
homo vulgaris. Yes, you'll know the face,

he is the one who answers truthfully
researchers' questionnaires, and it is he
who pays his union dues and doesn't run
for office; reads both *Telegraph* and *Sun.*

He knows the etymology of *berk*
so doesn't use the word; he likes his work.
A wife and rented house supply his need;
between them they'll perpetuate the breed.

Successive politicians court his votes;
the Antichrist, Computer, sifts his notes,
retrieves him under (Mr/Mrs/Miss)
abbreviated, in parenthesis.

More mouse than man's a judgement one might make,
a slow beginner, hardly yet awake—
but don't be misled, all's not as it seems:
he kills the fiercest dragons in his dreams

but holds his counsel, dumb against the day
he deems the time has come to have his say
and from the literati he'll reclaim
the wealth of poems written in his name.

The Sting

Wanted, on a charge of seditious libel contained in his
ironical work entitled '*The Shortest Way With The Dissenters*'
a reward of Fifty Pounds is offered for information leading
to the arrest of

Daniel Defoe

"*a middle-sized man about forty years old, brown complexion, dark
brown hair but wears a wig; a hooked nose, sharp chin, grey eyes; a
large mole near his mouth.*" (London Gazette, c1702)

I suppose the mole was a dead give-away,
and money talks—it always did—
fifty pounds would have bought more
than a lot of first editions
on Grub Street in those days.

Caught, sentenced, pilloried for three days.
But the crowds came not with stones
or foul abuse; rather with words of praise
and flowers to deck the pillory,
flasks to drink your health;

money, too, to buy your written works.
Your publishers set up stalls, stood by
with reprints, saying "What a turn-up
for the book. Better this, by far,
than any ordinary signing session!"

Amen to that—

and Robinson Crusoe yet to set sail from Hull;
it makes you proud.

Words

Against us all
who wrong you,
won't you fight
sometimes—
as the baited bull
uses horns
and skull,
when driven by pain
to retaliate—
fight back
you English words.

I know you:
you are regal as queens,
juicy as fruit,
carefree as gay,
as butch as a dame
in a man's suit;
chick as a girl,
or as queer
as the transvestite
in the heat
of the night.
It is strange how the thought
of a close-cut lawn
could lead
via grass
to smack or crack;
that a joint
can be bought
not to roast
but to smoke,
and a poke
could be other
than the bonnet once worn
by one's mother.

But it's tough
to know what is meant
by a puff,
and a bust
I'd decline
to define.

Fortify me
with some frankness
from York
whose flat-vowelled talk
has no frills,
from Grimsby and Clee
and old Ridings
where a spade stays a spade,
and invoices bills,
no less.
Let me sometimes stand
with you,
attack,
and turn my hand
against all whose aims
usurp your good names;
let us win back her wand
for the fairy.

LOVE STORIES

Epithalamium

We hadn't thought to meet again
so soon after that first glance,
mutually approving, in the pub
before the dance. Introduction
superfluous. *Tuxedo Junction. In the Mood.*

I overstayed my leave, then back
to barracks; a last few tedious months
and every day our letters,
each repeating a love
that neither knew the measure of.

Late summer and I came home
to stay, to shake out a future
from the given cardboard box—
gaberdine, double-breasted
grey pinstripe and all.

And all that September we watched
the leaves re-colour our secret wood,
and months later, on the bus
passing that place, you would press
your knee to mine, and it was as good.

Our wedding in April; the honeymoon.
Primroses from a Sussex wood
our epithalamium
pressed between cellophane sheets
in an album of fading fashions.

And so again to September, your dirndls
put away, the borrowed wrap-overs
letting out our secret
inch by flowered inch
to a brittle winter.

The burnished snow rejecting
my prints each evening
to your ward. Our firstborn.
The having, holding,
and the long, reluctant letting go.

All You Need Is Love

They bring their children now
to see us, over the rebuilt bridges.
Something delicate, potent, in the smell
of a child's skin, his hair,
transcends time and reason.

There is joy as well as hurt,
when he tires of our game,
in his well-aimed handful of toys.
It is a phase. There were always
phases, not to be talked about.

A son's first graffito, saying
little, but significant of much.
The mass of motorbikes, summonses;
rebellion pushing the clock past midnight;
callers in cars and quiet conversations.

Posters of Paul and John, guardant
over a daughter's bed, their music
closeting her away for hours,
all you need is love pounding the walls.
Horses; the cavalletti of puberty.

Grandad, the children say, *come
into the garden and play—and Grandma.*
We count slowly up to ten, then
set out in search of them, leave
their favourite places until last,

find precisely what it is we seek.
Asleep now in his mother's warmth,
'*Little Black Sambo*' fallen to the floor,
they carry him into the car and are
gone with the sun, over safe bridges.

We bring the house to order, replace
the ornaments, make another pot of tea,
and know that we shall ache all week
from games we played far less
for their sakes than for our own.

To My Wife . . .

Cloves round the ham I'd remember
and rosemary to flavour the beef.
You ask would I know how to manage
if you were the first one to die.
Manage the home? In a fashion, I'd say.
Routine? There'd be that in my life,
my goings to time and my coming back home
to find the same stillness I'd left behind
veneered with a whisper of dust.
My weekdays soothed by balsam of work.
Evenings stone-silent, only my own sad singing,
strident to reassure, just as in childhood
crossings of ghostly bedroom landings.

In our bedroom I should know cold comfort
and lonely sunbleached sheets, still
smelling the fresh-caught sea air—and you.
The bloodwarm underblanket wouldn't bring
our bed alive in love, or stilled in sleep,
and in the morning I would pour again for two,
forgetting; I'd flounder through the numbing days
to weekends' wifeless husbandry, coping,
cooking for only one reluctant appetite.
And then would be the hardest time to think,
to eat alone again, to think, and then again
the cloves round the ham I'd remember
and rosemary to flavour the beef.

Sonnet: Through Mother's Eyes

In celebration of the successful cornea-grafting operation
performed, shortly after mother's death, using her eyes in
the restoration of sight to someone unknown.

An ear for music, eye for pretty sights
were gifts she'd share with anyone who cared.
She gave a rhythm to the spoken word
and lent her eyes to brighten starless nights;
she saw life's colours, not mere blacks and whites,
perceived a peacock in the plainest bird,
lit optic beacons when her joy was stirred
by children's songs or colourbox delights.

She showed her gratitude in later years,
bequeathed her eyes that others might see still,
and I'm aware, as I soliloquize,
that though my words may fail to reach her ears,
by some coincidence—and surgeon's skill—
my poem might be read through mother's eyes.

Bacalao

Yesterday's boat brought a shark, hoisted
tail-over-snout above deck, tall, sleek
as stray cats scavenging the refuse bins;
sight-seers a mixed catch of language.

Today, the *Mar Celeste* has landed her fish
except these five kept by the crew for curing,
split, salted and spreadeagled between stays,
bacalao hung to the sun and the wind.

My father would have quickened to this,
envied these Mallorquin their climate,
criticised, enthused, pronounced judgement
based on a lifetime's curing of cod.

Splitting, pricking-up, laying out the fish
to dry, participles by which he lived;
he knew, by smell and feel of skin, a catch
from Iceland, White Sea, the Faroes.

Bacalao, he used to say, *a delicacy in Spain*,
steaming the biscuit-hard flakes, flavouring
the whole house, adding parsley; proving, if only
to himself, his work *food fit for a king*.

That One

But that was hardly
the gist of it,
family words with which
she cloaks herself,
holds sympathy at bay,

telling of good times,
peasantry and simple joys
helping a hard-worked husband
live long enough to see
the children grown.

She doesn't tell of one son
an occasional voice
on a far phone,
the birthday card, each year,
which seldom comes,

the woodwork jewellery box,
empty, on her dressing table,
his initials on the base
with 'upper Vth—1958'
she daily dusts.

Topping and tailing gooseberries
into her aproned lap—
he loves me, he loves me not—
she talks of summer thunder
souring the milk in the jug,

she doesn't tell of nights awake
willing the waning moon
to her room, her dream
falling like a stone
into the well of unknown.

Not That He Was Not Loved

Frame, son, the old man would say,
you're not framing up to the job.

And the lad, uncertain, struggled
with his father's verb to frame.

It was like that, his life, little came
simple to the son in the doing of it.

Not that he was not loved beyond a grief
for the young wife killed in his bearing.

Through the dry years and prayers since
fallen away from them, the son tried long

to please his father, working to draw
from him words he kept for his pigeons.

It was like that, his life, what little
came easily went without a word.

Now, wearing the old man's cast-off age,
framing, he hears again the voice only he

heard at the graveside, not the priest's
intoning, but the old man's directing

the paying out of strops, inching himself
to his place at her side: *frame now, frame.*

Polishing the old man's twelve-bore he wonders
if at last he could master that verb.

Son

There are the quiet times, too,
when somehow I almost forget

this aching awareness of you,
your absences, sullen, prolonged

departures from the way we planned
piecing together the parallels

of model railway track, debating bends;
and how often, at golf, we'd drive

into opposite rough, disdaining
the fairway, to pincer the green

and halve, in six, an easy par-four;
or, fishing the wide bay, your rod

to port and mine angled starboard,
each of us riding his obstinate swell,

our tackles tangled under the boat,
snagged paternosters in conflict

tightened ambivalent lines—
just as it was with my father.

Anniversary

But then, with age, it's not at all like that,
there's not the fight to keep the fire alight
there was when we were young; and now tonight
the ash of years perpetuates the heat,
and love's become a comfortable grate
by which to sit, touch hands to consummate.

No more the backing smoke, eye-smarting haze,
or panic caused by roaring chimney fires.
Burnt out by now the vicious, spitting coals;
no bubbling hiss of tarry will-o-wisps.
A graceful, ballet-skirted glow remains
to dance the hearth's slow-burning of the days.

To think that, years ago, these coals were trees
and slender saplings wrestled with wild winds,
bowed low, sprang back and scratched the seasons' eyes
and suffered in each other's restlessness,
then, in full time, stood proud with summer's pods,
and now their progeny our favourite woods.

Today we walk through winter trees, and by
the trackside, skeletal against the sky
the silver birch, its lace all stripped away,
splendid in sunlight, seems to us to say:
though greens that autumn browned are gone today,
touch, feel my bark, the warmth is here to stay.

The Gazebo

Today I awoke early, restless, refusing the last
dark drops from the dugs of sleep, impatient
for the day as a mule to slip its spancel,
yet not wanting to listen again to the words

I'd heard so many times—like numbers for the rugby
league cup draw shaken in their velvet bag,
picked out in random order—always the same words.
Presentation handshake, photograph I'll likely never see,

and this final homeward journey, earlier than usual.
The books are closed. My desk, its drawers now empty,
will face tomorrow from a slightly different angle
with someone else's photograph in place of yours.

It is good, alone in the car, to savour homecoming;
the road seems to have shed its sense of urgency.
Combines have come like carrion crows to bloat
on the fattening feast; the hedgerow throws a cloak

over the place where poppies spilled their blood.
Two men with a theodolite read the field's palm,
predict a meeting with the motorway next year.
A long and happy retirement, he said. They clapped.

I heard partridge rising, shot them down with words.
You will want to know how it was; I shall have time
to tell. And while I'm telling we shall keep
one eye to the future, looking for new roads.

Rest will not contain us both for long, and if time
and fate should sometimes make us weak we shall strive,
like the skylark rising, for a song of noble note,
dip our minds into new colours in the woods again.

Too soon now I steer the car under the prunus arch
into the drive. *Piacevole,* carved in Lombardic at
the outset of our journey, weathered now but bold.
Petunias play tubas in the sawn-off buttertub.

You meet me home. We walk into the garden, sit on
the long seat and share a silent gathering of strength.
We'll have tea on the lawn, perhaps, and talk of endings
and beginnings, and one of us will fall asleep.

Tomorrow we shall blow dust off old plans. There
will be York stone to cut, edges crisp as cinder-toffee.
You will serve a brave new recipe for lunch. And after,
we shall build the gazebo where our dreams are stored.

This Day Dawning

This day dawning is the black fruitgum,
the sixpence in the pudding; the day
dad first let go the bicycle's saddle.
It is my mother's knee, the ease
when the toothache had gone.

It is the day I was appointed—
and the day I was released.
It is every bill in the house paid off.
This day is cyclamen and holly
dancing to a daffodil band.

It is the day when Olive said *yes*.
Bubbles in a baby's bath, balloons
and his first bouncing words.
It is the day my son returned home;
my daughter singing in the choir.

It is the Christmas stockings filled;
the tightly rolled-up fiver
in the Salvation Army tin.
Top hat and tails and taxis
and that first successful waltz.

It is Pickering Park and Costello;
one magnificent minnow
in a jam jar bright with rainbows.
It is the uncashed cheque for one guinea
for a first ever poem in print.

This day dawning is the taste returning
after a bout of heavy cold.
It is the irresistible invitation
of a vast untrodden snow
and only I can put my foot in it.

Love Story

Their wedding holds firm
in its frame on the wall—
above the gravid shelves
of Bainbridge, Yevtushenko—
the frontispiece
of an ageing book.

Take down their tome
and read how forty years
taught tolerance, timing,
routine—even *ad libs*
are polished with practice,
though their style is spare.

Barely a word they waste
and their silences
say more for them.
Apart, they are closer
than together, knowing by heart
each other's conflating rôle;

she, in the kitchen,
slicing and halving the loaf
—diagonally on Sundays—
Mondays, giving the house
and him no rest,
blowing out her gale;

he, in the garden shed,
chewing an endless cud
of self-control, feeding
a rodent anger,
poulticing with pastimes
the unspent rage of his youth.

Evenings, a shared synopsis,
a tautology of sighs . . . .
And now their kiss goodnight
asks no new question,
makes no fresh statement
as would its absence.

Their story's not yet over—
leave them in this lacuna,
put their book back on its shelf
beneath the faded photo
of two young lovers—
each watching the other grow old.